Auld Acquaintances

Auld Acquaintances
❦ Famous Music from the James Fuld Collection

J. Rigbie Turner

Preface by Charles E. Pierce, Jr.

Foreword by James Fuld

The Pierpont Morgan Library

Auld Acquaintances: Famous Music from the James Fuld Collection
is a record of an exhibition held at The Pierpont Morgan Library,
New York, from 24 May through 27 August 1995.

Copyright © 1995 by The Pierpont Morgan Library. All rights reserved.

Published in 1995 by
The Pierpont Morgan Library
29 East 36th Street
New York, New York 10016

ISBN 0-87598-110-0

All photography by David A. Loggie.
Designed and printed by the Oliphant Press.

Front cover and frontispiece: The first printing of
the words and music together of *Auld Lang Syne*, 1799.
Back cover: James Fuld's bookplate.

Preface

Charles E. Pierce, Jr.
Director, The Pierpont Morgan Library

I do not recall precisely when I first met James Fuld. Most likely, it was shortly after I became Director in September 1987. But I do recall precisely the occasion upon which he and I first discussed the possible acquisition of his collection by the Library and a possible exhibition of some of his greatest treasures at the Library. It was during the summer of 1989, over lunch at Gloucester House. By this time, I knew that Mr. Fuld by vocation was a lawyer, having been a managing partner of Proskauer Rose Goetz & Mendelsohn, and that by avocation he was a collector of first editions of famous pieces of printed European and American music. I knew, furthermore, that his collection was the most important of its kind in private hands and that it was unique in its depth and diversity. And I knew that he was an influential scholar in the field of music bibliography, having written numerous articles and two indispensable reference books.

What I did not know, but soon discovered, was his passion for his collection, his respect for the Morgan Library, and his desire that his collection remain intact and reside in the fullness of time in a great research library, where it could be studied by scholars and enjoyed by the public. What I also did not know, but rapidly came to appreciate in the discussions that followed, was how fair-minded, thoughtful, and generous of spirit Mr. Fuld is. It was a happy day when the Trustees of the Library agreed to purchase this collection, for through this single act the music collection of the Morgan Library will become infinitely greater. To its own extraordinary collection of autograph music manuscripts will be added this extraordinary collection of European and American printed music. The Morgan Library, which is already a musical mecca, will thus become more than ever a place to which all serious scholars, composers, conductors, and performers will want to make their way.

It was also a happy day when Mr. Fuld, J. Rigbie Turner, the Mary Flagler Cary Curator of Music Manuscripts and Books, and I agreed that we should organize an exhibition to highlight some of the true treasures from this great collection. This was not an easy task. But it was a challenge that both Mr. Fuld and Mr. Turner took up with pleasure as they sought to demonstrate the range, quality, rarity, and condition of the collection as a whole. They have chosen to exhibit only 200 items out of a possible 10,000. They have created one exhibition; they could have created many more. I am pleased by what they have done, and I thank them for their efforts. I am especially grateful to Mr. Fuld for all that he has done to bring this collection and this exhibition to the Library. And I am thankful to Mr. Turner for having brought the exhibition and this publication into being. I wish also to acknowledge the help of the following Library staff members: William Appleton, Noah Chasin, David Coleman, Mary Cropley, Patricia Emerson, Julianne Griffin, Timothy Herstein, David A. Loggie, Marilyn Palmeri, Patricia Reyes, Edward J. Sowinski, Fredric Woodbridge Wilson, and Deborah Winard. I am proud that the Morgan Library can now share with the public some of the most famous and best preserved pieces of printed music ever created in Europe and America.

Foreword

James Fuld

It all started innocently.

I grew up in the "golden age" of American music—the late 1920s and 1930s, when Gershwin, Kern, Berlin, Porter, and Rodgers were composing—and I played their songs on the piano as soon as they appeared. I quickly began collecting first editions of earlier famous American songs as well, eventually turning to a wide spectrum of well-known classical, popular, and folk music of all kinds and from many countries, 1567 to present.

People have long been interested in early or original written or printed works. Aristotle collected ancient manuscripts, and a Shakespeare first folio ranks among the world's most highly prized objects. Famous musical works as they first came into the world are fascinating to me. Aside from their historic significance, first editions can be intrinsically valuable if the original manuscript does not survive or if the composer made changes to the work during its printing. To identify an original edition required that I spend a great deal of time in American, European, and Soviet archives examining the first editions of classical, popular, and folk music.

These original editions have broadened my interests, and the collection includes autographs of celebrated composers, librettists and lyricists, performers, publishers, musicologists, and collectors; original librettos and literary sources of operas; programs and posters for musical events in which eminent composers or performers participated; contemporary newspaper references; other ephemera of historic note associated with ballet, jazz, opera houses, and pianos; mise-en-scènes; music illustrated by noted artists; early phonograph and piano roll recordings of prominent composers; as well as portraits, medals, visiting cards, bookplates, tickets, stamps, batons, and porcelain objects. Nevertheless, the original editions of widely recognized musical works form the core of the collection.

It has been fun to have assembled this collection of about 10,000 original editions of well-known music and related items over the past 65 years.

It is particularly gratifying that The Pierpont Morgan Library, in my home city, desires, and will one day permanently acquire, the entire collection. I deeply thank Charles E. Pierce, Jr., Director, and J. Rigbie Turner, Mary Flagler Cary Curator of Music Manuscripts and Books, for their interest and support.

On James Fuld and *Auld Acquaintances*

J. Rigbie Turner
Mary Flagler Cary Curator of Music Manuscripts and Books

On 3 January 1974, James Fuld wrote a letter to Herbert Cahoon at the Morgan Library. It began: "Would your Library be interested in an Exhibit of '1st Printings of Well-Known Music'? I know of no such previous exhibit, and I have not suggested it before.... If this may be of interest to you, perhaps you and Mr. Turner might like to see the music and consider it further?" Mr. Cahoon was curator of autograph manuscripts at the Library; I, the assistant curator. Mr. Cahoon has since retired; I am now curator of music manuscripts; and Mr. Fuld, with this exhibition, sees a suggestion of two decades standing fulfilled. Although parts of the Fuld collection have been shown before, this is the first major exhibition devoted to Mr. Fuld's holdings—by all accounts the greatest private collection of printed music in the world.

Most collectors have several traits in common: They are patient, inquisitive, and discriminating; they may relish the chase almost as much as the capture but can be zealous in their attachment to their treasures; they set realistic goals, knowing full well they cannot have everything. That it requires a certain amount of money to be a successful collector goes without saying; but it is also true that vast expenditures will not in themselves produce a good, or even mediocre, collection. Many who spend small fortunes on their hoards are not true collectors, only buyers.

Another conviction shared by collectors is that some objects of the past, distant or recent, are worth preserving. Why save first editions of music? Because they document works as they first saw the light of day, allowing us to study symphonies, operas, and songs as the composer issued them—without the layers of editorial accretions with which they often subsequently become burdened. The first edition does not, of course, tell the scholar or performer all he needs to know about a work; the diligent researcher will go back to the autograph manuscript (if it survives) and forward to editions corrected or revised by the composer. But if no original or copyist's manuscripts survive, the first edition assumes a heightened authority and may well be the only primary source for a composition.

As they acquire objects, true collectors, of necessity, learn a great deal about them. Some keep their findings to themselves, while others (sometimes grudgingly) pass on their wisdom to the rest of us. Few collectors, however, display Mr. Fuld's generosity of spirit, and fewer still his willingness—no, eagerness—to share his information and the genuine pleasure his avocation provides. Over the years he has corresponded with librarians and bibliographers around the world, dazzled countless visitors in his score-lined living and dining rooms, and published two books—*The Book of World-Famous Music* and *The Book of World-Famous Libretti*—that belong at the elbow of every librarian, collector, dealer, and musicologist. (A list of Mr. Fuld's writings on music appears on pp. 47–48.)

Auld Acquaintances is what curators call a treasures show—one that is all peaks and no troughs, all stars and no bit players. As such it has no theme, tells no story, and is not a history of anything. It was planned to demonstrate the depth and range of the Fuld collection, its variety and strengths, its mixture of the familiar and the unusual. We hope this is fairly conveyed but must acknowledge the rigorous limitations of this objective: Choosing a few hundred items from the 10,000 or so in the collection meant leaving out countless candidates worthy of inclusion in any treasures show. Faced with this embarrassment of riches, the challenge was first "What *must* we include?" and then "Which many thousands *must* we leave out?" To that end, each item has been chosen with care and often was included to represent one of the many genres the collection comprises: primarily musical first editions but also librettos, programs, posters, autographs, mise-en-scènes, recordings, photographs, bookplates, and ephemera.

Even the casual observer will notice the absence of many well-known composers—Albéniz, Bruckner, Corelli, and Donizetti for starters. They were omitted not because Mr. Fuld owns no first editions of their music (he does) but simply because there was no room for them. Bear in mind, too, that most composers who have been included are represented by a single item, even though in nearly every instance there were many options. Thus a few Bach, Mozart, or Beethoven items must stand for his outstanding holdings of those three composers; and his vast collection of Berlin, Kern, Porter, Gershwin, and Rodgers sheet music in first edition is only hinted at by a handful of songs. Put another way, these 200 or so objects—a core collection the envy of any dealer and the pride of any collector—amount to perhaps 2 percent of Mr. Fuld's holdings.

These items were chosen to enlighten, to entertain, and occasionally to surprise. Among the surprises encountered, at least by this seeker of curiosities, are the following:

~ *Three Blind Mice* was first published in 1609—the same year as Shakespeare's *Sonnets* and that in which Henry Hudson sailed up the tidal estuary that one day would be called the Hudson River.

~ The melody we know as *Twinkle, Twinkle, Little Star* was first published, in Paris, in 1774—the year in which Louis XVI began his reign with his queen, Marie-Antoinette.

~ The first printed reference to Beethoven, in 1783, also mentions Bach and Mozart, thus linking the three gods in Mr. Fuld's musical pantheon.

~ The first printing of the words and music together of *Auld Lang Syne* was in 1799, when Beethoven was working on his First Symphony.

~ The melody of *Frère Jacques* was first published in 1811, the same year as Beethoven's *Emperor* Piano Concerto.

~ The two most familiar wedding marches, those by Mendelssohn and Wagner, were published within a few years of one another.

~ Liszt's *Liebestraum*, one of the most famous piano pieces ever written, was originally composed as a song.

~ The music of *The Marines' Hymn* is by Jacques Offenbach; it was first published in 1868, the same year as Brahms's *Wiegenlied* (Lullaby) and Wagner's *Meistersinger von Nürnberg*—which are also represented in the exhibition.

~ The melody of the "Habanera" from *Carmen* is not by Bizet but was based on a song by Sebastián Yradier (to whom Bizet gave credit when the piano-vocal score was published in 1875).

~ We actually know the composer of *Happy Birthday to You*—probably the most frequently sung music in this country—although it has all but become a folk song in the century since it was first published.

~ Hoagy Carmichael's *Star Dust*, one of the most recorded songs ever, was originally published not as a song but as a piano solo, and the familiar opening words of the chorus—"Sometimes I wonder why I spend the lonely night"—were added later and are not even by the composer.

~ Gershwin's "The Man I Love"—Mr. Fuld's favorite song by his favorite American composer—was dropped during the pre-Broadway tryout of *Lady, Be Good!* (1924), the musical for which it was written. It was sung (as "The Girl I Love") in *Strike Up the Band* (1927), a show that closed out of town; added and then cut before the pre-Broadway tryout of *Rosalie* (1928); and rejected when *Strike Up the Band* was successfully revived in 1929 because the song had become too popular. In the rare first edition of the sheet music, the title is misprinted *The Man I Loved*.

We trust that visitors will happen on some surprises of their own and have no doubt that they will see many auld acquaintances—and a few unfamiliar faces—in this exhibition.

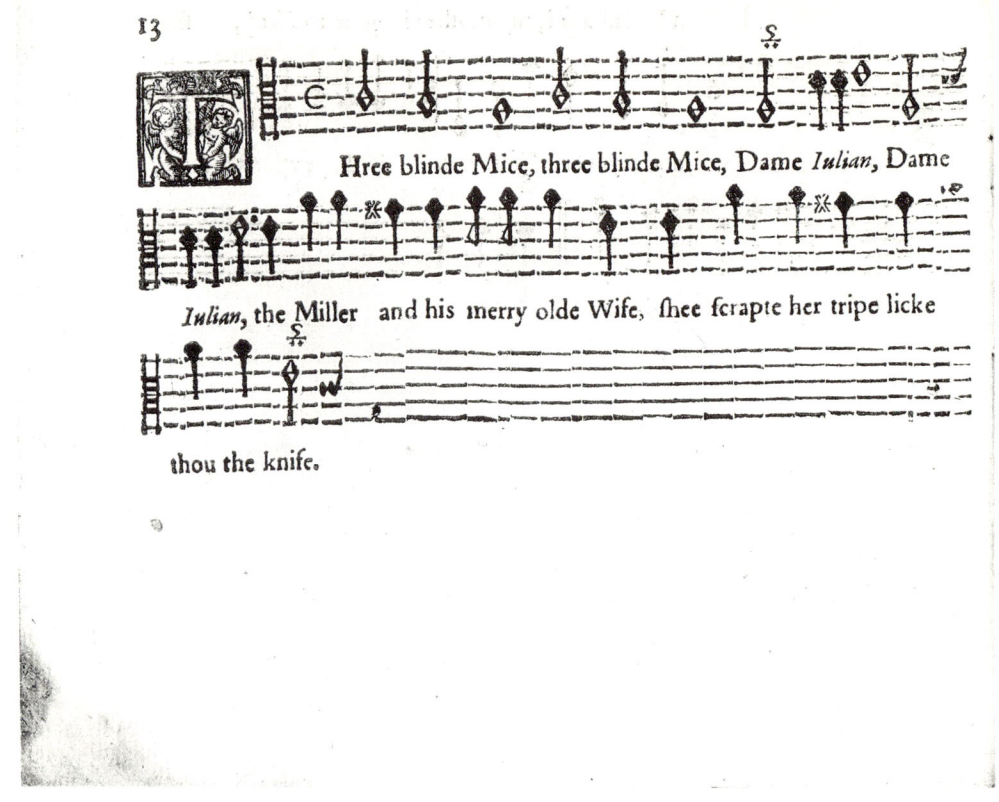

FIG. 1. *The first printing of* Three Blind Mice, *1609*

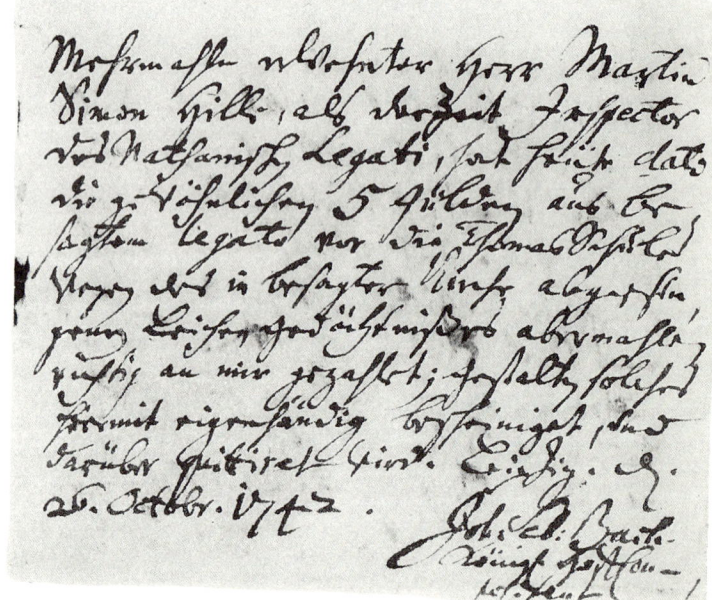

FIG. 2. *An autograph receipt signed by J. S. Bach, 1742*

🌿 Checklist

This checklist is divided into three sections: Classical Music, American Popular and Folk Music (both shown in the Exhibition Room), and Foreign Popular and Folk Music (shown in the Cloister).

Several special cases highlight items that we consider especially noteworthy.

🌿 Classical Music
Case Exhibits

Giovanni Pierluigi da Palestrina
1525 or 1526–94

Missa Papae Marcelli   *Joannis Petri Aloysi* [sic] *Praenestini Missarum liber secundus.* Rome: Eredi di Valerio & Aloysio Dorico, 1567. Contains what is believed to be the only virtually complete copy in this country of the first edition of the *Missa Papae Marcelli* (Pope Marcellus Mass), perhaps the most famous musical work of the Renaissance.

Claudio Monteverdi
1567–1643

Il qvinto libro de madrigali a cinqve voci . . . Col basso continuo per il clauicembano [sic] *chittarone od altro simile istromento . . . Di nuouo ristampato.* Venice: Ricciardo Amadino, 1608. Third printing of the Basso part.

Thomas Ravenscroft
ca. 1582–ca. 1635

Three Blind Mice   *Deuteromelia: or The second part of musicks melodie, or melodius musicke.* London: printed for Thomas Adams, 1609. Contains the first printing of *Three Blind Mice.* Although this is obviously not a "classical" composition, it is included to show the widely diverse music available during this early period (fig. 1).

Antonio Vivaldi
1678–1741

The Four Seasons   *Il cimento dell'armonia e dell'inventione concerti a 4 e 5 . . . Opera ottava libro primo* [and *secondo*]. Amsterdam: Michele Carlo Le Cene, 1725. First edition of the first violin part of the twelve concertos op. 8. The first four concertos—"La primavera," "L'estate," "L'autunno," and "L'inverno"—are popularly known as *The Four Seasons.*

Johann Sebastian Bach
1685–1750

"Goldberg" Variations   *Clavier Ubung bestehend in einer Aria mit verschiedenen Veraenderungen vors Clavicimbal mit 2 Manualen.* Nürnberg: Balthasar Schmid, 1742. First edition of the *Goldberg* Variations, one of the few works by Bach published during his lifetime.

Passionsmusik . . . nach dem Evangelium Matthaei Cap. 26 und 27. Berlin: J. G. Brüschcke, 1829. The libretto for Felix Mendelssohn's performances of the *St. Matthew Passion* on 11 and 21 March 1829.

Autograph document signed, dated Leipzig, 26 October 1742, a receipt for 5 gulden from Martin Simon Hille (fig. 2).

George Frideric Handel *1685–1759*	*Messiah, an oratorio.* London: Tho. Wood, 1743. The only known copy of Charles Jennens's libretto for the first performance of *Messiah* in London, on 23 March 1743.
	A clipping from an unidentified London newspaper noting a performance of *Messiah* conducted by Handel; the concert was in the Foundling Hospital Chapel, probably on 18 April 1751.
Christoph Willibald Gluck *1714–87*	*Orfeo ed Euridice azione teatrale per musica . . . Rappresentata in Vienna, nell' anno 1764.* Paris: Duchesne, 1764. First edition of the full score.
Daines Barrington *1727–1800*	*Miscellanies.* London: J. Nichols, 1781. First edition; contains Barrington's essay on Mozart, "Account of a Very Remarkable Young Musician," preceded by an engraved portrait of Mozart at the age of seven (fig. 3).
Wolfgang Amadeus Mozart *1756–91*	*Sei quartetti per due violini, viola, e violoncello. . . . Opera X.* Vienna: Artaria & Comp., 1785. First edition of the parts of the *Haydn* Quartets, K. 387, 421/471b, 458, 428/421b, 464, and 465, which includes the famous dedicatory letter to Haydn.
	Autograph sketch, K. 626b/12.
	Le nozze di Figaro. Comedia per musica tratta dal francese in quattro atti. Da rappresentarsi nel Teatro di corte l'anno 1786. Vienna: Giuseppe Nob. de Kurzbe[c]k, 1786. First edition of the libretto by Lorenzo da Ponte.
	Medal (1796).
Joseph Haydn *1732–1809*	**"Surprise" Symphony** *Sinfonie à grand orchestre . . . Œuvre 80me.* Offenbach: J. André; Amsterdam: J. H. Henning, 1795. First edition of the parts for the *Surprise* Symphony (H. I:94).
Ludwig van Beethoven *1770–1827*	**"Moonlight" Sonata** *Sonata quasi una fantasia per il clavicembalo o piano=forte . . . Opera 27. N° 2.* Vienna: Gio. Cappi, 1802. First edition of the *Moonlight* Sonata.
	(See also *Special Case*, below.)
Franz Schubert *1797–1828*	**Ave Maria** *Sieben Gesänge aus Walter Scott's Fräulein vom See in Musik gesetzt mit Begleitung des Pianoforte . . . Op. 52.* Vienna: Math. Artaria, 1826. Contains the first edition of *Ave Maria* (D. 839).
	"Unfinished" Symphony *Zwei Sätze der unvollendeten Sinfonie (in H moll) . . . Nachgelassenes Werk. Partitur.* Vienna: C. A. Spina, 1867. First edition of the full score of the *Unfinished* Symphony (D. 759).

Η σοι γ'εκ γενεης τα δαμ' εσπετο θαυματα εργα;
Η ε τις αθαναΊων, ηε θνηΊων ανθρωπων
Δωρον αγαυον εδωκε, και εφρασε θεσπιν αοιδην;

                                        HOMER'S Hymn on Mercury.

FIG. 3. *An engraved portrait, published in 1781, of Mozart at the age of seven*

Gioachino Rossini *1792–1868*	**The Barber of Seville** overture *Gran sinfonia nell'opera Aureliano in Palmira . . . ridotta per forte-piano dal Sig.ʳ Maestro Francesco Bojle.* Milan: Gio. Ricordi, 1814. First edition of the piano arrangement of the overture Rossini first used in *Aureliano in Palmira* (1813), then in *Elisabetta, regina d'Inghilterra* (1815), and finally in *Il barbiere di Siviglia* (1816).
Carl Maria von Weber *1786–1826*	Medal (1825).
Frédéric Chopin *1810–49*	*Sonate pour le piano . . . Œuv. 35.* Leipzig: Breitkopf & Härtel, 1840. First German edition, which was published simultaneously with the French.
Robert Schumann *1810–56*	**Träumerei** *Kinderscenen. Leichte Stücke für das Pianoforte . . . Op. 15.* Leipzig: Breitkopf & Härtel, 1839. Contains the first edition of *Träumerei*.
Franz Liszt *1811–86*	*Liebesträume. 3 notturnos für das Pianoforte.* Leipzig: Fr. Kistner, 1850. First edition.
Felix Mendelssohn-Bartholdy *1809–47*	**"Wedding March"** *Ein Sommernachtstraum von Shakespeare . . . Op. 61. Partitur.* Leipzig: Breitkopf & Härtel, 1848. First edition of the full score of the incidental music, which includes the "Wedding March."
Richard Wagner *1813–83*	**"Wedding March"** *Lohengrin romantische Oper in drei Akten . . . Vollständiger Klavierauszug von Theodor Uhlig.* Leipzig: Breitkopf & Härtel, 1851. First edition of the piano-vocal score, which includes the "Wedding March." [*Die Meistersinger von Nürnberg.* Mainz: B. Schott's Söhne, 1868.] Printed proof sheets of the first edition of the piano-vocal score of Acts II and III with numerous corrections, some in Wagner's hand. Wagner stamp (1889).
Charles Gounod *1818–93*	**Ave Maria** *Méditation sur le Iᵉʳ prélude de piano de S. Bach, composée pour piano et violon solo, avec orgue ad lib.* Paris: Heugel et Cie., 1853. First edition of the melody that was later set to words as *Ave Maria*.
Giuseppe Verdi *1813–1901*	*Rigoletto melodramma di F. M. Piave . . . Riduzioni per canto con accomp. di pfte. . . . di Luigi Truzzi.* Milan: Giovanni Ricordi, 1852. First complete edition of the piano-vocal score.
Victor Hugo *1802–85*	*Le Roi s'amuse, drame.* Paris: Eugène Renduel, 1832. First edition of the play that was the source for Verdi's *Rigoletto*.

Edvard Grieg *1843–1907*	*Concert für Pianoforte mit Begleitung des Orchesters... Op. 16. Partitur.* Leipzig: E. W. Fritzsch, 1872. First edition of the full score of the Piano Concerto.
Johannes Brahms *1833–97*	**Wiegenlied** *Lieder und Gesänge mit Begleitung des Pianoforte.* Berlin: Simrock, 1868. First edition of the songs, op. 49, including *Wiegenlied* (Lullaby).
Ruggero Leoncavallo *1857–1919*	*Pagliacci dramma in due atti parole e musica di R. Leoncavallo.* Milan: Edoardo Sonzogno, 1892. First edition of the piano-vocal score.
Modest Petrovich Musorgsky *1839–81*	*Khovanshchina.* Autograph album leaf for piano (without voice) with the first 15 measures of Scene 6 (Act V, Scene 1, in Rimsky-Korsakov's version).
Pyotr Il'yich Tchaikovsky *1840–93*	**The Nutcracker** [Cover:] [*P. Chaykovskiy Shchelkunchik balet'-feeriya*] *Op. 71.* [Title page:] *Casse-noisette ballet-féerie en 2 actes... Op. 71. Gr. partition d'orchestre.* Moscow: P. Jurgenson, 1892. First edition of the full score of *The Nutcracker.*
Arnold Schoenberg *1874–1951*	*Verklärte Nacht Sextett für zwei Violinen, zwei Violen und zwei Violoncelli Op. 4... Partitur.* Berlin: Verlag Dreililien, 1905. First edition of the score of *Transfigured Night.* With a program of Schoenberg conducting the version for string orchestra; Vienna, Mittlerer Konzerthaus-Saal, 25 February 1924.
Antonín Dvořák *1841–1904*	*Aus der neuen Welt. "Z nového světa." Symphonie (N° 5, E moll.) für grosses Orchester... Op. 95. Partitur.* Berlin: N. Simrock, 1894. First edition of the full score of the Symphony no. 9 *(From the New World).* With Anton Seidl, autograph musical quotation (from this symphony) signed, dated New York, 23 March 1894.
Claude Debussy *1862–1918*	*Pelléas et Mélisande drame lyrique en 5 actes et 12 tableaux de Maurice Maeterlinck.* Paris: A. Durand & fils, 1902. The issue of *Le Théatre,* no. 84 (June 1902), with photographs of the sets and singers.
Gustav Mahler *1860–1911*	*Symphonie N° 5 für grosses Orchester... Partitur.* Leipzig: C. F. Peters, 1905. First edition of the full score of the Symphony no. 5.
Igor Stravinsky *1882–1971*	**The Firebird** [*Zhar'-ptitsa skazka-balet v 2-kh kartinakh'. Sostavil po russkoy narodnoy skazke Mikhail Fokin'... Fortepiano v 2 ruki.*] *L'Oiseau de feu conte dansé en 2 tableaux. Composé d'après le conte national russe par M. Fokine... Piano à 2 mains.* Moscow: P. Jurgenson, 1910. First edition of *The Firebird* arranged for piano. Inscribed by the composer, with a musical quotation, to James Fuld.

The Rite of Spring *Le Sacre du printemps tableaux de la Russie païenne en deux parties d'Igor Strawinsky et Nicolas Roerich réduction pour piano à quatre mains par l'auteur.* Berlin: Édition Russe de Musique, 1913. First edition of Stravinsky's arrangement of *The Rite of Spring* for piano four hands.

Sergey Diaghilev
1872–1929

Autograph letter signed, dated St. Petersburg, 31 October 1900, to an unidentified recipient; the letterhead was designed by Léon Bakst.

Vaclav Nijinsky
1888–1950

Autograph sentiment signed, [no place, no date], reading *Dansons, prions, aimons* (Let us dance, pray, love).

Charles E. Ives
1874–1954

Second pianoforte sonata "Concord, Mass., 1840–60." Redding: Charles E. Ives, 1920. First edition of the *Concord* Sonata, printed for the composer.

Alban Berg
1885–1935

Georg Büchners Wozzeck Oper in 3 Akten (15 Szenen) ... op. 7 Klavierauszug von Fritz Heinrich Klein Eigentum des Komponisten. Vienna: Alban Berg, 1923. First edition of the piano-vocal score, privately published by Berg.

Maurice Ravel
1875–1937

Bolero ... Partition d'orchestre. Paris: Durand & Cie., 1929. First edition of the full score of *Boléro*.

George Gershwin
1898–1937

Rhapsody in Blue for jazz band and piano ... piano solo and second piano. New York: Harms Incorporated, 1924. First edition of the arrangement for two pianos, inscribed by the composer to Max Abramson.

Sergey Prokofiev
1891–1953

Peter and the Wolf [*Soch. 67 Petya i volk simfonicheskaya skazka dlya detey perelozheniye dlya fortepiano avtora*] ... *Op. 67 Pierre et le loup conte symphonique pour enfants réduction pour piano par l'auteur.* Moscow: Muzgiz, 1937. First edition of the piano score of *Peter and the Wolf.*

Dmitry Shostakovich
1906–75

Op. 47 [*Pyataya simfoniya*] *Cinquième symphonie* [*dyla bol'shogo orkestra*] *pour grand orchestre* [*Partitura*] *Partition d'orchestre.* Moscow: Gosudarstvennoye Muzïkal'noye Izdatel'stvo, 1939. First edition of the full score.

Aaron Copland
1900–90

Autograph musical quotation signed from *Fanfare for the Common Man.*

John Cage
1912–92

4'33". New York: Henmar Press, 1960. Early edition. In his instructions for performing this work, in which the player(s) remain silent, Cage writes that it "may be performed by any instrumentalist(s) and the movements may last any lengths of time."

🎵 Classical Music Wall Exhibits

Joseph Haydn *1732–1809*	Playbill for a concert that included a "Simphonie de Haydn"; Brussels(?), unidentified hall, 28 April 1786.
Two music publishers	Johann Gottlob Immanuel Breitkopf (1719–94). Autograph letter signed, dated [n.p., Leipzig], 12 April 1760, to Reich. Domenico Artaria (1765–1823). Autograph document signed, dated Vienna, 10 March 1794, mentioning portraits of Haydn.
Four tickets	1684 (copper), 1769 (silver), [1772] (paper), and 1794 (ivory).
Frédéric Chopin *1810–49*	Playbill for Chopin's first concert in Paris, at the "salons de MM. Pleyel et Cie.," dated 25 February 1832 (the concert was postponed and held on 26 February).
Vincenzo Bellini *1801–35*	*Norma.* Poster for an early performance; Milan, La Scala, 15 May 1834.
Hector Berlioz *1803–69*	Playbill for Berlioz's first concert in Vienna; Theater an der Wien, 16 November 1845.
Franz Liszt *1811–86*	Playbill for a concert; London, Theatre Royal, Covent Garden, 2 June 1827.
Nicolò Paganini *1782–1840*	Playbill for a concert; London, Theatre Royal, Drury Lane, 17 July 1833.
Richard Wagner *1813–83*	*Tristan und Isolde.* Playbill for the first performance; Munich, Königliches Hof- und Nationaltheater, 10 June 1865 (fig. 4). *Siegfried.* Engraved music plate of p. 100 from Act I, Scene 3, of the first edition of the full score. Mainz: B. Schott's Söhne, 1875.
Giuseppe Verdi *1813–1901*	*Il trovatore* and *Rigoletto* (as *Viscardello*). Poster for early performances; Forlì, Teatro Comunale, 1853 (pl. 1).
Johannes Brahms *1833–97*	Piano Quartet no. 1 in G minor. Program for the first performance; Hamburg, Kleiner Wörmerscher Saal, 16 November 1861. Clara Schumann played the piano part, and, with Brahms, played Mozart's Sonata for Two Pianos in D, K. 448. Program for a concert that included Brahms performing Beethoven's Piano Concerto no. 5 (*Emperor*); Vienna, Gesellschaft der Musikfreunde, 8 November 1874.

FIG. 4. *A playbill for the first performance of Wagner's* Tristan und Isolde, *1865*

Nicholas II, czar of Russia
1868–1918

Program for a gala performance at the Bolshoi Theater (Moscow) on 17 May 1896, following the coronation of Czar Nicholas II.

Giacomo Puccini
1858–1924

La Bohème. Poster for the original production; Turin, Teatro Regio, 1896 (pl. 2).

Gustave Charpentier
1860–1956

Louise. Poster for the original production; Paris, Opéra-Comique, 1900.

Enrico Caruso
1873–1921

Photograph and self-caricature, each signed and dated New York, 1907.

Modest Petrovich Musorgsky
1839–81

Boris Godunov. Poster for a performance with Chaliapin et al.; Paris, Opéra, 4 June 1908.

Richard Strauss
1864–1949

Der Rosenkavalier. Poster for the first performance; Dresden, Königliches Opernhaus, 26 January 1911.

Giacomo Puccini
1858–1924

Turandot. Poster for the first performance, conducted by Arturo Toscanini; Milan, La Scala, 25 April 1926 (pl. 3).

Béla Bartók
1881–1945

Piano Concerto no. 1. Playbill for a performance of the concerto, with the composer as soloist, conducted by Nicolas Slonimsky; Paris, Salle Pleyel, 21 February 1932.

George Gershwin
1898–1937

Porgy and Bess. Program for the first performance; Boston, Colonial Theatre, 30 September 1935 (with the stub of James Fuld's ticket from the opening night; fig. 5).

Arturo Toscanini
1867–1957

Poster for a concert with the NBC Symphony Orchestra; Carnegie Hall, 22 February [1941]. With a baton used by Toscanini.

Leonard Bernstein
1918–90

Program for a concert by The Philharmonic-Symphony Society of New York; Carnegie Hall, 14 November 1943. Bernstein replaced an indisposed Bruno Walter at the last minute, after the program had been printed.

Maria Callas
1923–77

Poster of Callas in *La traviata*; Milan, La Scala, 5 February 1956.

Visiting cards

Brahms, Caruso, Debussy, Grieg, Haydn, Liszt, Mahler, Massenet, Paganini, Puccini, Rimsky-Korsakov, J. Strauss II, Stravinsky, Toscanini, Verdi, and Wagner.

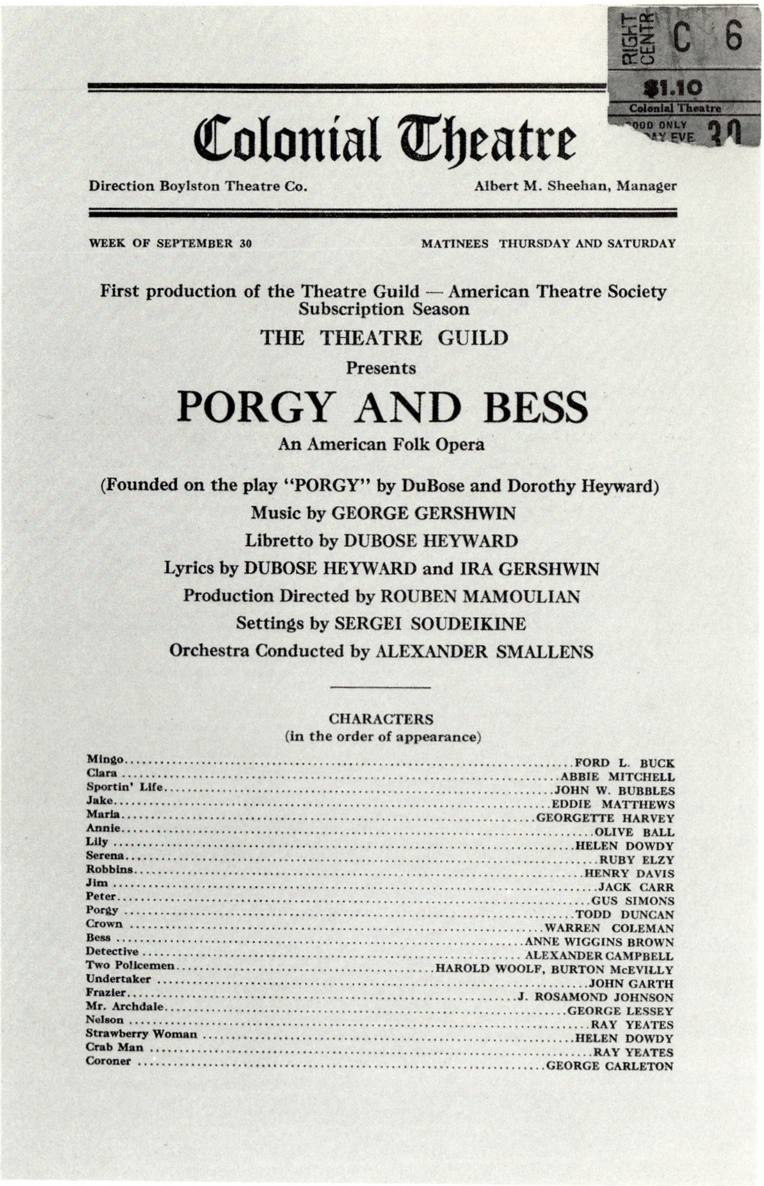

RIGHT CENTR C 6
$1.10
Colonial Theatre

Colonial Theatre

Direction Boylston Theatre Co. — Albert M. Sheehan, Manager

WEEK OF SEPTEMBER 30 — MATINEES THURSDAY AND SATURDAY

First production of the Theatre Guild — American Theatre Society
Subscription Season

THE THEATRE GUILD

Presents

PORGY AND BESS

An American Folk Opera

(Founded on the play "PORGY" by DuBose and Dorothy Heyward)

Music by GEORGE GERSHWIN

Libretto by DUBOSE HEYWARD

Lyrics by DUBOSE HEYWARD and IRA GERSHWIN

Production Directed by ROUBEN MAMOULIAN

Settings by SERGEI SOUDEIKINE

Orchestra Conducted by ALEXANDER SMALLENS

CHARACTERS
(in the order of appearance)

Mingo	FORD L. BUCK
Clara	ABBIE MITCHELL
Sportin' Life	JOHN W. BUBBLES
Jake	EDDIE MATTHEWS
Maria	GEORGETTE HARVEY
Annie	OLIVE BALL
Lily	HELEN DOWDY
Serena	RUBY ELZY
Robbins	HENRY DAVIS
Jim	JACK CARR
Peter	GUS SIMONS
Porgy	TODD DUNCAN
Crown	WARREN COLEMAN
Bess	ANNE WIGGINS BROWN
Detective	ALEXANDER CAMPBELL
Two Policemen	HAROLD WOOLF, BURTON McEVILLY
Undertaker	JOHN GARTH
Frazier	J. ROSAMOND JOHNSON
Mr. Archdale	GEORGE LESSEY
Nelson	RAY YEATES
Strawberry Woman	HELEN DOWDY
Crab Man	RAY YEATES
Coroner	GEORGE CARLETON

FIG. 5. *A program for the first performance of Gershwin's* Porgy and Bess *(with the stub of James Fuld's ticket from the opening night), 1935*

PL. 1. *A poster for early performances of Verdi's* Il trovatore *and* Rigoletto *(here called* Viscardello*), 1853*

PL. 2. *A poster for the original production of Puccini's* La Bohème, *1896*

PL. 3. *A poster for the first performance of Puccini's* Turandot, *1926*

***** Article of Agreement. *****

This agreement entered into this 10th day of August in the year of our Lord 1899 by and between John Stark and son party of the first part and Scott Joplin party of the second part both of the City of Sedalia and County of Pettis and State of Missouri.

Witnesseth: That whereas Scott Joplin has composed a certain piece of music entitled Maple Leaf Rag and has not funds sufficient to publish same it is hereby agreed with above parties of the first part that John Stark and son shall publish said piece of music and shall pay for all plates and for copy right and printing and whatevr may be necessary to publish said piece of music.

It is further agreed by and between the parties hereto that John Stark and son shall have the exclusive right to said piece of music to publish and s sell and handle the same as they may seem fit and proper to their interest.

It is further agreed by and between the parties hereto that Scott Joplins name shall appear in print on each and every piece of music as composer and John Stark and son as publishers.

It is further agreed by and between the parties hereto that Scott Joplin shall have free of charge ten copies of said piece of music as soon as published.

It is further agreed by and between said parties that Scott Joplin the composer of said music shall have and recieve a royalty of one cent per copy on each copy of said piece of musi sold by said Stark and son.

It is further agreed by and between said parties that the said Scott J Joplin shall be allowed to purchase and the said Stark and son agrees to sell to the said Joplin all the copies of said music he may want at the price of Five cents per copy, said copies shall not be sold for less than Twent-five cents per copy by said Joplin. It is further agreed that John Stark & Son will not retail for less than Twenty five cents per copy.

Witness our hands and seals the day and year first above written.

John Stark & Son
Scott Joplin

Signed in presence of
R A Higdon

PL. 4. *The original contract for the publication of Scott Joplin's* Maple Leaf Rag, *1899*

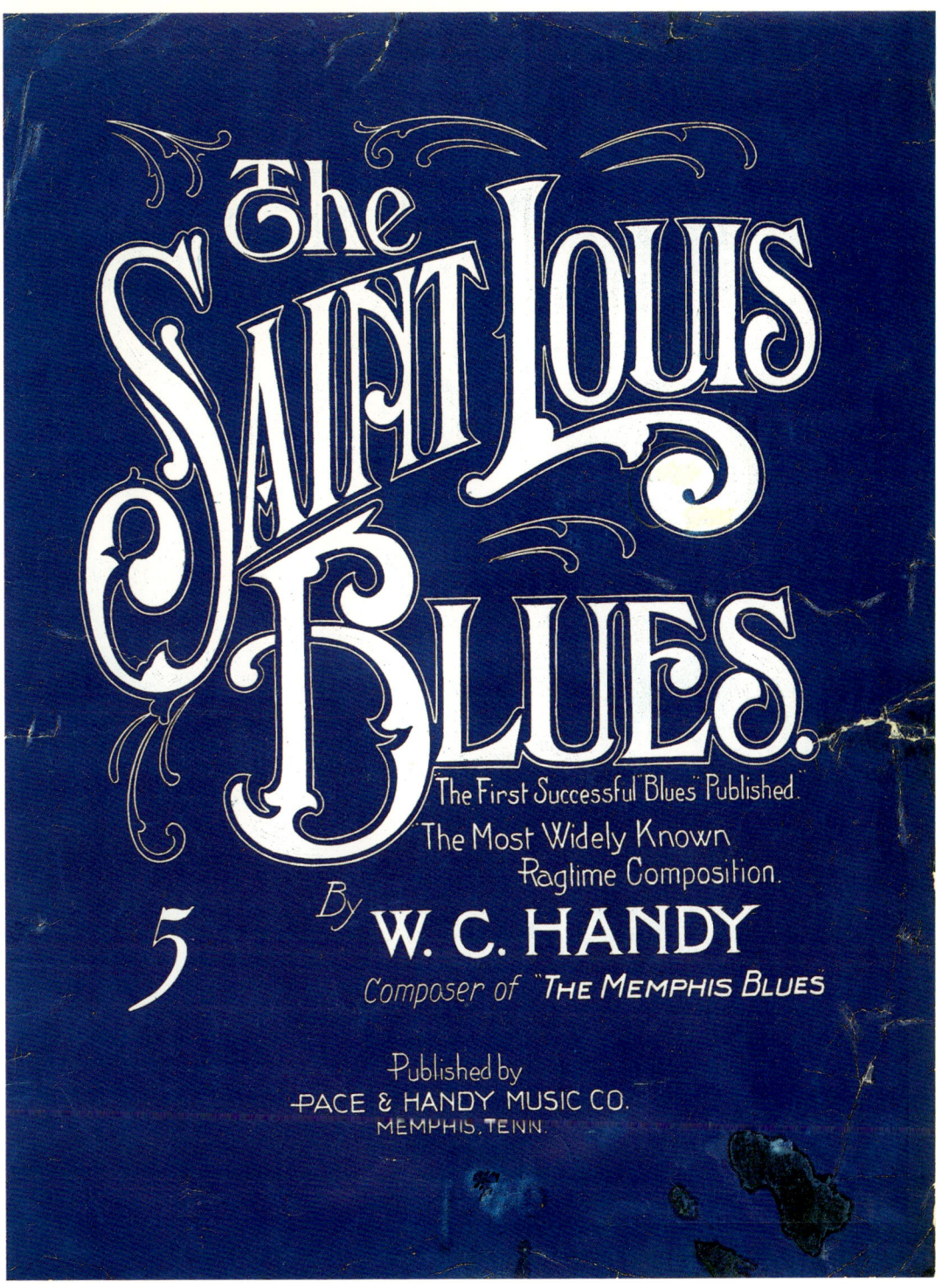

PL. 5. *The first edition of W. C. Handy's* Saint Louis Blues, *1914*

PL. 6. *The first edition of* Bill *by Jerome Kern and P. G. Wodehouse, 1918*

PL. 7. *A poster for the original Broadway production of Rodgers and Hammerstein's* Carousel, *1945*

PL. 8. *The alternative first edition of Johann Strauss II's* Blue Danube Waltz *arranged for piano, 1867*

PL. 9. *Franz Xaver Gruber's* Vier ächte Tyroler-Lieder, *which contains the first edition of* Silent Night, *1832*

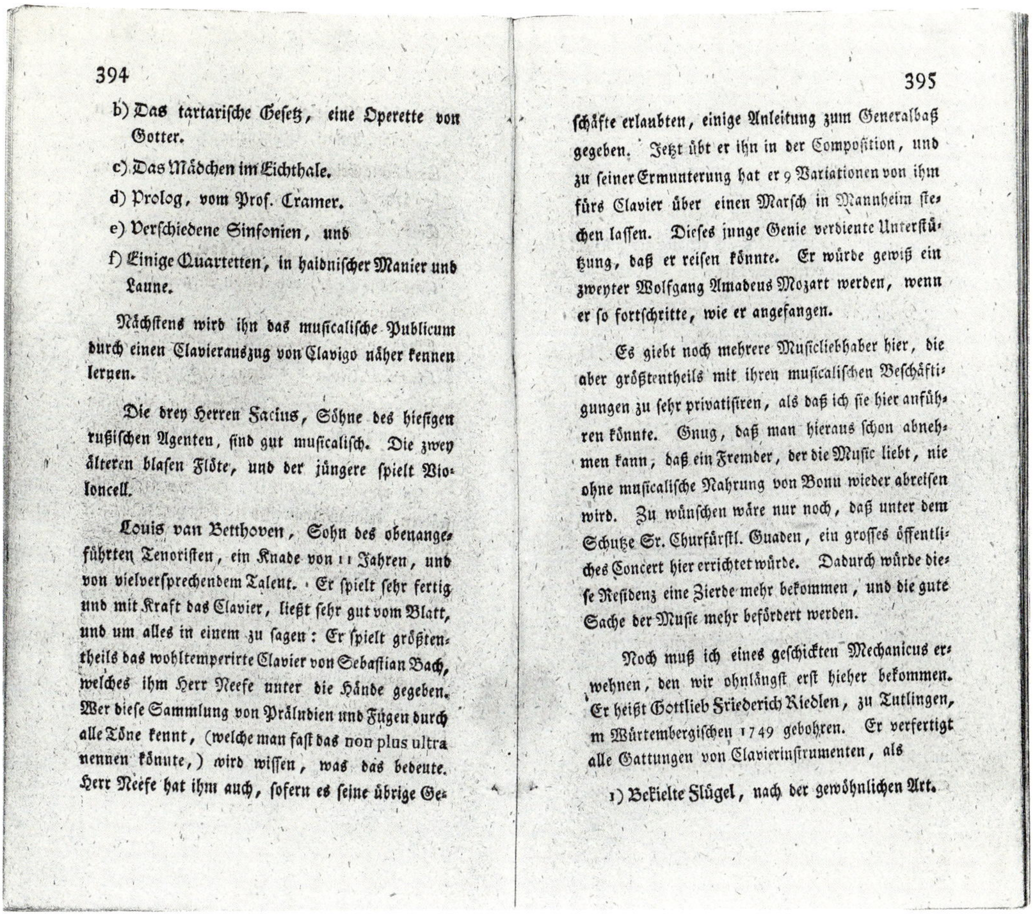

394

b) Das tartarische Gesetz, eine Operette von Gotter.

c) Das Mädchen im Eichthale.

d) Prolog, vom Prof. Cramer.

e) Verschiedene Sinfonien, und

f) Einige Quartetten, in haidnischer Manier und Laune.

Nächstens wird ihn das musicalische Publicum durch einen Clavierauszug von Clavigo näher kennen lernen.

Die drey Herren Facius, Söhne des hiesigen rußischen Agenten, sind gut musicalisch. Die zwey älteren blasen Flöte, und der jüngere spielt Violoncell.

Louis van Betthoven, Sohn des obenangeführten Tenoristen, ein Knabe von 11 Jahren, und von vielversprechendem Talent. Er spielt sehr fertig und mit Kraft das Clavier, ließt sehr gut vom Blatt, und um alles in einem zu sagen: Er spielt größtentheils das wohltemperirte Clavier von Sebastian Bach, welches ihm Herr Neefe unter die Hände gegeben. Wer diese Sammlung von Präludien und Fugen durch alle Töne kennt, (welche man fast das non plus ultra nennen könnte,) wird wissen, was das bedeute. Herr Neefe hat ihm auch, sofern es seine übrige Ge-

395

schäfte erlaubten, einige Anleitung zum Generalbaß gegeben. Jetzt übt er ihn in der Composition, und zu seiner Ermunterung hat er 9 Variationen von ihm fürs Clavier über einen Marsch in Mannheim stechen lassen. Dieses junge Genie verdiente Unterstützung, daß er reisen könnte. Er würde gewiß ein zweyter Wolfgang Amadeus Mozart werden, wenn er so fortschritte, wie er angefangen.

Es giebt noch mehrere Musicliebhaber hier, die aber größtentheils mit ihren musicalischen Beschäftigungen zu sehr privatisiren, als daß ich sie hier anführen könnte. Gnug, daß man hieraus schon abnehmen kann, daß ein Fremder, der die Music liebt, nie ohne musicalische Nahrung von Bonn wieder abreisen wird. Zu wünschen wäre nur noch, daß unter dem Schutze Sr. Churfürstl. Gnaden, ein grosses öffentliches Concert hier errichtet würde. Dadurch würde diese Residenz eine Zierde mehr bekommen, und die gute Sache der Music mehr befördert werden.

Noch muß ich eines geschickten Mechanicus erwehnen, den wir ohnlängst erst hieher bekommen. Er heißt Gottlieb Friederich Riedlen, zu Tutlingen, im Würtembergischen 1749 gebohren. Er verfertigt alle Gattungen von Clavierinstrumenten, als

1) Bekielte Flügel, nach der gewöhnlichen Art.

FIG. 6. *The first printed reference to Beethoven, which also mentions Bach and Mozart, 1783*

Special Case

Ludwig van Beethoven *1770–1827*

Beethoven, Bach, Mozart *Magazin der Musik. Herausgegeben von Carl Friedrich Cramer . . . Erster Jahrgang, 1783.* Hamburg: Musicalische Niederlage, 1783. Contains the first printed reference to Beethoven, in an article by Christian Gottlob Neefe that mentions the young Beethoven's playing of Bach's *Well-Tempered Clavier* and ends: "He would surely become a second Wolfgang Amadeus Mozart were he to continue as he has begun." (This is James Fuld's favorite item in the collection; fig. 6.)

[Symphony no. 7, op. 92. Vienna: S. A. Steiner, 1816.] First edition of the full score (possibly a proof copy), lacking the title and dedication pages. This is the only known copy with all of the original printing errors—at least twenty-five on the first page alone.

A sketch for the second movement of the Symphony no. 7. Shown with Sieghard Brandenburg's transcription.

❧ American Popular and Folk Music Case Exhibits

Philo Leeds
b. 1702/03

Philo Leeds, His Book, Annadominy 1733. Manuscript in one or two hands. Contains "An Introduction To all Lovers of Psalmody," "For The Flute," etc. This is believed to be the second-earliest known American music manuscript.

Thomas Johnston
1708–67

[Collection of psalm tunes.] Boston: Thomas Johnston, 1755. First edition (incomplete); compiled, engraved, printed, and published by Johnston.

Anon.

The Liberty Song   *Bickerstaff's Boston Almanack, for the Year of our Lord 1769.* Boston: printed by Mein and Fleeming, and to be sold by John Mein, 1768. Contains the first printing of the words and music together of *The Liberty Song*, the first patriotic music to be published in America (fig. 7).

[Alexander Reinagle
1756–1809]

Fœderal March as performed in the grand procession in Philadelphia the 4th of July 1788 composed and adapted for the piano forte, violin or German flute. [Philadelphia: sold by John Aiken, 1788.] First edition of the earliest illustrated American sheet music.

[Philip Phile
d. 1793]

Hail Columbia   *The Favorite New Federal Song adapted to the Presidents March.* [Philadelphia: Benjamin Carr, 1798.] First edition of the song that soon became known as *Hail Columbia*, America's first (if unofficial) national anthem; the words are by Joseph Hopkinson.

Anon.

Yankee Doodle. New York: Printed & Sold at J. Hewitt's Musical Repository, 1798. Early American edition of the song, the first to be printed with words. The authorship of both words and music is unknown.

[James Hewitt
1770–1827]

The Battle of Trenton a sonata for the piano-forte dedicated to General Washington. New York: Printed & sold by James Hewitt at his musical repository, 1797. First edition, which has a particularly handsome front cover.

FIG. 7. *The first printing of the words and music together of* The Liberty Song, *1768*

Lowell Mason 1792–1872, ed.	**My Country! 'Tis of Thee** *The Choir: or Union collection of church music. Consisting of a great variety of psalm and hymn tunes, anthems, &c. . . .* Boston: Carter, Hendee and Co., 1832. Contains the first printing of the music and words (five stanzas) together of *America*, later published as *My Country! 'Tis of Thee*. The words are by Samuel Francis Smith.
Anon.	*Battle Hymn of the Republic adapted to the favorite melody of "Glory, Hallelujah," written by Mrs. Dr. S. G. Howe, for the Atlantic Monthly.* Boston: Oliver Ditson & Co., 1862. First edition of the song. The words are by Julia Ward Howe; the composer of the music is not known.
Clarence Augustus Barbour 1867–1937, ed.	**America the Beautiful** *Fellowship Hymns.* New York: Young Men's Christian Association Press, 1910. Contains the first known printing of the words and music together of *America the Beautiful*. The words are by Katharine Lee Bates, and the music is by Samuel A. Ward.

George M. Cohan *1878–1942*	*Over There.* New York: William Jerome Publishing Corporation, 1917. Early edition of the song, signed by the composer.
Irving Berlin *1888–1989*	"God Bless America." Autograph manuscript signed of the words of the song; [New York, 1940].
[Jacques Offenbach *1819–80*]	**"From the halls of Montezuma"** *The Marines* [sic] *Hymn.* New York: Printed but not published by U.S.M.C. Publicity Bureau, 1918. First known edition of the song. The music is by Jacques Offenbach; the author of the words, which begin "From the halls of Montezuma," is not known.
Louis Moreau Gottschalk *1829–69*	Autograph musical quotation signed, dated Buffalo, 24 March 1862. With a photograph of Gottschalk.
Stephen C. Foster *1826–64*	*Stay Summer Breath favorite ballad.* Louisville: W. C. Peters & Co., 1848. First edition of the song, inscribed by the composer (with initials) to Sallie S. McCormick; the only known inscribed copy of a Foster work. **"Way down upon the Swanee River"** *Old Folks at Home Ethiopian melody as sung by Christy's Minstrels written and composed by E. P. Christy.* New York: Firth, Pond & Co., 1851. First edition of the song. Because Foster had sold the song to Christy, his name does not appear on the music.
Anon.	**The Bonnie Blue Flag** (Confederate version) *The Bonnie Blue Flag composed, arranged, and sung at his Personation Concerts by Harry Macarthy.* New Orleans: A. E. Blackmar & Bro., 1861. Possible first edition of the song. Macarthy wrote the words; the composer of the music is not known.
[Dan Emmett *1815–1904*]	**Dixie** *I Wish I Was in Dixie song by W. H. Peters Esq. music by J. C. Viereck.* New Orleans: P. P. Werlein, 1860. One of three known copies of the first (unauthorized) edition of the music of *Dixie* (fig. 8).
Minstrel pitcher	A ceramic pitcher with pictures of nine minstrel performers and the titles of two songs, "I Wish I Was in Dixay Land" and "Sally Is the Only Girl for Me." Manufactured in July 1870, probably by Minton & Co. (Stoke-on-Trent, England).
James Pierpont *1822–93*	**Jingle Bells** *The One Horse Open Sleigh.* Boston: Oliver Ditson & Co., 1857. First edition of the song. *Jingle Bells or The One Horse Open Sleigh.* Boston: Oliver Ditson & Co., 1859. Second edition of the song.

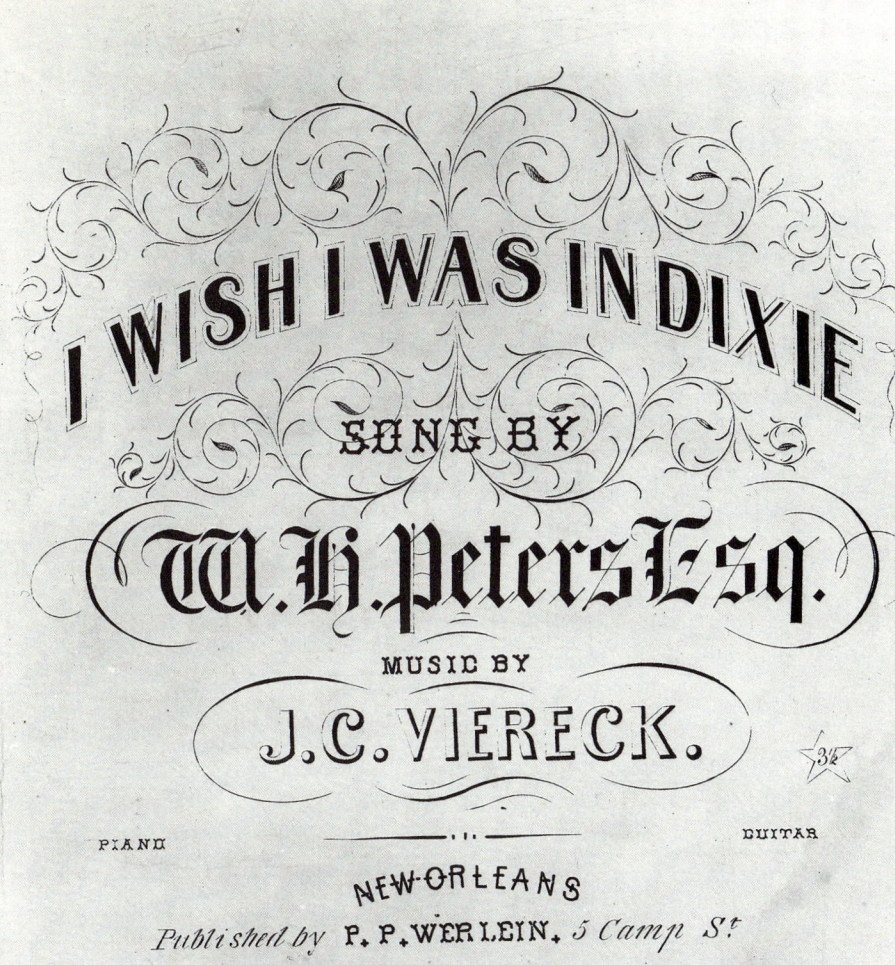

FIG. 8. *The first (unauthorized) edition of the music of Dan Emmett's* Dixie, *1860*

Anon.	**Go Down, Moses** *The song of the "Contrabands" "O Let my people Go" words and music, obtained through the Rev. L. C. Lockwood.* New York: Horace Waters, 1861. First known edition of *Go Down, Moses*, the first African-American spiritual to appear in print that is still well known.

Anon.	**Columbia, the Gem of the Ocean** *Columbia the Land of the Brave written and composed by David T. Shaw . . . arranged by T. A. Beckett Esq.* Philadelphia: George Willig, 1843. First edition of the song; in 1844 it was renamed *Columbia, the Gem of the Ocean*. The authorship of both words and music is unknown.

Septimus Winner
1827–1902	**Listen to the Mocking Bird** *Sentimental Ethiopian ballad. Listen to the Mocking Bird melody by Richard Milburn written and arranged by Alice Hawthorne.* Philadelphia: Winner & Shuster, 1855. First edition of the song. The melody is by Milburn; Alice Hawthorne was one of Winner's pseudonyms.

Henry Randall Waite
1845–1909, compiler	**Mary Had a Little Lamb** *Carmina collegensia: a complete collection of the songs of the American colleges, with piano-forte accompaniment. . . .* Boston: Oliver Ditson & Co., 1868. Contains the first known printing of the words and music together of *Mary Had a Little Lamb*. The words are by Sarah J. Hale; the music is elsewhere credited to E. P. Christy.

John Philip Sousa
1854–1932	Autograph musical quotation signed from *The Stars and Stripes Forever!* dated 1920.

Mildred J. Hill
1859–1916	**Happy Birthday to You** *Song Stories for the Kindergarten. Music composed and arranged by Mildred J. Hill. Words written and adapted by Patty S. Hill.* Chicago: Clayton F. Summy, 1893. Contains *Good-morning to All*, the first printing of the music that later became *Happy Birthday to You* (fig. 9).

Anon.	**We Shall Overcome** *I'll Overcome Someday featured by Kenneth Morris and the Martin & Morris Gospel Singers original words by Atron Twigg revised lyrics and music by Kenneth Morris.* Chicago: Martin & Morris Music Studio, [1946?]. Early edition of the gospel song, one of several sources for *We Shall Overcome*.

Albert Von Tilzer
1878–1956	**Take Me Out to the Ball Game** *The sensational base ball song Take Me Out to the Ball Game words by Jack Norworth.* New York: The York Music Co., 1908. First regular edition of the song, signed by the composer with a musical quotation.

Henry W. Armstrong
1879–1951	**Sweet Adeline** *Sweet Adeline ballad & refrain. Words by Richard H. Gerard.* New York: M. Witmark & Sons, 1903. First edition of the song, signed by the composer, with a musical quotation.

FIG. 9. *The first printing of the music that later became* Happy Birthday to You, *1893*

Anon.	*Missouri Waltz from an original melody procured by John Valentine Eppel . . . arranged for piano by Frederic Knight Logan.* Chicago: F. J. A. Forster, 1916. The first edition with the words by J. R. Shannon. Inscribed by Harry S. Truman.
Scott Joplin 1868–1917	**Maple Leaf Rag** The original contract between Joplin and the publisher John Stark & Son for the publication of Joplin's *Maple Leaf Rag*, dated Sedalia, Mo., 10 August 1899 (pl. 4).
	The Entertainer *The Entertainer a rag time two step.* St. Louis: John Stark & Son, 1902. First edition; for piano.
W. C. Handy 1873–1958	*The Saint Louis Blues.* Memphis: Pace & Handy, 1914. First edition, signed by Handy (pl. 5).
Duke Ellington 1899–1974	*Harmony in Harlem.* 78 rpm recording (Brunswick 8044), signed by Ellington.

Cotton Club	Program for "Cotton Club on Parade," featuring Cab Calloway; undated.
Benny Goodman *1909–86*	Signed photograph.
Richard Rodgers *1902–79*	"Some Enchanted Evening," from *South Pacific*. Words by Oscar Hammerstein II. New York: Williamson Music Inc., 1949. First edition of the sheet music, signed by the composer.
George Gershwin *1898–1937*	["The Man I Love," from *Lady, Be Good!*] Autograph manuscript signed of the melody and inner voicing of the song, written out for the violinist Paul Kochański. The manuscript includes two other songs, one unpublished.
	"The Man I Love," from *Lady, Be Good!* Lyrics by Ira Gershwin. New York: Harms Incorporated, 1924. One of two known copies of the first edition of the song with the misprint *The Man I Loved* on the front cover.
	"I Got Rhythm," from *Girl Crazy*. Lyrics by Ira Gershwin. New York: New World Music Corp., 1930. First edition of the sheet music.
Irving Berlin *1888–1989*	*Alexander's Ragtime Band.* New York: Ted Snyder Co., 1911. First edition of the song, inscribed by the composer to James Fuld.
	"Easter Parade," from *As Thousands Cheer*. Lyrics and music by Irving Berlin. New York: Irving Berlin, Inc., 1933. First edition of the sheet music, signed by Berlin.
Jerome Kern *1885–1945*	"Ol' Man River," from *Show Boat*. Lyrics by Oscar Hammerstein II. New York: T. B. Harms, 1927. One of two known copies of the first edition of the sheet music.
	"Bill," from *Oh, Lady! Lady!!* Book and lyrics by Guy Bolton and P. G. Wodehouse. New York: T. B. Harms, 1918. First edition of the song, a revised version of which was later used in *Show Boat* (pl. 6).
	Kern's bookplate.
Cole Porter *1891–1964*	"Night and Day," from *Gay Divorce*. Music and lyrics by Cole Porter. New York: Harms Incorporated, 1932. First edition of the sheet music, signed by Porter.
Harold Arlen *1905–86*	"Over the Rainbow," from *The Wizard of Oz*. Lyrics by E. Y. Harburg. New York: Leo Feist, 1939. First edition of the sheet music, signed by Arlen and Harburg.

Richard Rodgers *1902–79*	*Away We Go!* Program for a pre-Broadway performance of *Oklahoma!* under its original title; Boston, Colonial Theatre, March 1943.
Arthur Schwartz *1900–84*	"Dancing in the Dark," from *The Band Wagon*. Lyrics by Howard Dietz. New York: Harms Incorporated, 1931. First edition of the sheet music, inscribed by the composer, with a musical quotation, to James Fuld.
Hoagy Carmichael *1899–1981*	*Star Dust.* New York: Mills Music, Inc., [1930?]. Possible first edition, for piano; signed by the composer with a musical quotation. (The words, by Mitchell Parish, were added later.)
Vincent Youmans *1898–1946*	*No, No Nanette.* Book and lyrics by Otto Harbach and Frank Mandel; additional lyrics by Irving Caesar. New York: Harms Incorporated; London: Chappell & Co., Ltd., 1925. First edition of the piano-vocal score.
Frank Loesser *1910–69*	*Guys and Dolls.* Music and lyrics by Frank Loesser. London: Edwin H. Morris & Co., Ltd., 1953. First edition of the piano-vocal score, signed by the composer.
Leonard Bernstein *1918–90*	*West Side Story.* Lyrics by Stephen Sondheim. New York: G. Schirmer, Inc., and Chappell & Co., Inc., 1959. First edition of the piano-vocal score, inscribed by the composer, with a musical quotation, to James Fuld. With a program for the pre-Broadway production; Washington, D.C., National Theatre, September 1957.
Marvin Hamlisch *b. 1944*	*A Chorus Line.* Program for the pre-Broadway production; New York, Public Theatre, 1975.
Vernon Duke *1903–69*	"April in Paris," from *Walk a Little Faster*. Lyrics by E. Y. Harburg. New York: Harms Incorporated, 1932. First edition of the sheet music, inscribed by the composer to James Fuld and signed by Harburg.
Jerry Bock *b. 1928*	"Sunrise, Sunset," from *Fiddler on the Roof.* Lyrics by Sheldon Harnick. New York: Sunbeam Music Corp., 1964. First edition of the sheet music. With a program for the original Broadway production; New York, Imperial Theatre, November 1964, signed by Zero Mostel.
Stephen Sondheim *b. 1930*	Autograph musical quotation signed from "Send in the Clowns," from *A Little Night Music.*
Frederick Loewe *1901–88*	*My Fair Lady adapted from Bernard Shaw's "Pygmalion" . . . book and lyrics by Alan Jay Lerner.* New York: Chappell & Co., Inc., 1956. First edition of the piano-vocal score, signed by Loewe (with a musical quotation) and Lerner.

American Popular and Folk Music Wall Exhibits

Christy Minstrels	Playbill; Boston, Ordway Hall, week of 9 April 1855.
John Philip Sousa *1854–1932*	*El Capitan.* Poster for the original production; [Boston, Tremont Theatre, 1896].
Marian Anderson *1897–1993*	Poster for her farewell tour, 1964–65.
Louis Armstrong *1900–71*	Poster for a performance at the Rhythm Club (New Orleans), 22 October 1944.
New Orleans Jazz and Heritage Festival	Poster; the performers included Duke Ellington, Al Hirt, Mahalia Jackson, and Pete Fountain; Municipal Auditorium & Beauregard Square, April 1970.
Dorsey brothers	Poster featuring Tommy and Jimmy Dorsey. The top of the poster, where the name of the theater and date of performance could be added as needed, is blank.
Al Jolson *1886–1950*	Signed photograph. With a still showing Jolson and May McAvoy in *The Jazz Singer.*
Count Basie *1904–84*	Poster; Bristol, Colston Hall, 13 February [n.y.].
Jerome Kern *1885–1945*	*Roberta.* Original movie poster; 1935.
Richard Rodgers *1902–79*	*Carousel.* Poster for the original Broadway production; [New York, Majestic Theatre, 1945] (pl. 7).
Irving Berlin *1888–1989*	*Top Hat.* Original movie poster; 1935.
Cole Porter *1891–1964*	*Kiss Me, Kate.* Poster for the original Broadway production; New York, New Century Theatre, 1948.
Irving Berlin *1888–1989*	*This Is the Army.* Poster for the original Broadway production; New York, Broadway Theatre, 1942.
	Annie Get Your Gun. Poster for the original Broadway production; New York, Imperial Theatre, 1946.

Richard Rodgers *Oklahoma!* Poster for the original Broadway production; New York, St.
1902–79 James Theatre, 1943.

Frederick Loewe *My Fair Lady.* Poster for the original Broadway production; New York,
1901–88 Mark Hellinger Theatre, 1956.

Jo Mielziner Color sketch labeled *School Framed Hanger* for the original production
1901–76 of Rodgers and Hammerstein's *The King and I,* dated 1950.

Leonard Bernstein *West Side Story.* Poster for the original Broadway production; New York,
1918–90 Winter Garden Theatre, 1957.

Elvis Presley Signed photograph.
1935–77

Woodstock *Woodstock Music and Art Fair presents An Aquarian Exposition. 3 Days of Peace and Music.* Poster for the Woodstock festival, August 1969. With a one-day ticket to the festival.

Special Cases

Anon. **Auld Lang Syne**   *A select collection of original Scotish* [sic] *airs for the voice . . . [Third] set.* London: printed and sold by Preston, 1799. First edition; contains the first printing of the words and music together of *Auld Lang Syne.* The authorship of the music and the first stanza of the text is unknown; the remaining words are by Robert Burns (frontispiece).

John Stafford Smith **The Star-Spangled Banner**   *The Anacreontic Song as sung at the
1750–1836 Crown and Anchor Tavern in the Strand the words by Ralph Tomlinson Esqr. late President of that Society.* London: Longman & Broderip, probably 1779–80. The first printing of the music that would become *The Star-Spangled Banner.*

The Star Spangled Banner, a pariotic [sic] *song.* Baltimore: Printed and sold at Carrs Music Store, 1814. One of only ten known copies of the first printing of the song that would become our national anthem. The words are by Francis Scott Key (fig. 10).

FIG. 10. *The first printing of* The Star-Spangled Banner, *1814*

Foreign Popular and Folk Music
Case Exhibits

Thomas Sternhold
d. 1549, compiler

Old Hundredth *The whole booke of psalmes, collected into englishe meter by Thomas Sternh. Iohn Hopkins and others, conferred with the Hebrue, with apt notes to sing them withall.* London: John Day, 1576. Contains an early printing of *Old Hundredth* ("All people that on earth do dwell").

Anon.

Greensleeves *The Dancing=Master: or, directions for dancing country dances, with the tunes to each dance for the treble-violin. The eleventh edition corrected; with all the additions of new dances and tunes, the whole printed in the new character.* London: printed by W. Pearson for H. Playford, 1701. Contains an early printing of the melody of *Greensleeves*.

[Charles de Lusse
1720–25?–after 1774,
compiler]

Twinkle, Twinkle, Little Star *Recueil de romances historiques, tendres et burlesques, tant anciennes que modernes, avec les airs notés. Par M. D. L**.* [Paris: no publisher], 1767 and 1774. Volume 2 contains *La Confidence naive*, the first known printing of the words and music together of the song beginning *Ah! vous dirai-je, maman*—later, inter alia, *Twinkle, Twinkle, Little Star*.

Anon.

Drink to me only with thine eyes. A favorite glee for three voices. London: Printed for Babb's Musical Circulating Library, ca. 1780. One of several early, possibly first, printings of the melody, the authorship of which is unknown. The words are by Ben Jonson.

Thomas Augustine Arne
1710–78

Rule Britannia *The music in The judgment of Paris. Consisting of all the songs, duettos and trio, with the overture, in score...To which...are added the celebrated ode, in honour of Great-Britain, call'd Rule Britannia... Opera sesta.* London: Henry Waylett, ca. 1745. First edition; contains the first printing of the music and words together of *Rule Britannia*.

[Alexey Fyodorovich L'vov
1798–1870]

Czarist Russian national anthem [*Pesn ruskikh', "Bozhe tsarya khrani!" dlya khora s akkompanimentom fortepiyano.*] St. Petersburg: K. Pets, ca. 1833. Probable first printing of the first Russian national anthem, as composed for chorus; neither L'vov nor Vasily Andrevich Zhukovsky, who wrote the words, is mentioned.

Anon.

The East Is Red *Songs of New China.* Peking: Foreign Language Press, 1953. First edition; contains the possible first printing of *The East Is Red*, a folk song that has virtually been adopted as the national anthem of the People's Republic of China.

Pierre Capelle **Frère Jacques** *La clé du caveau à l'usage de tous les chansonniers*
1772–1851, compiler *français, des amateurs, auteurs, acteurs du vaudeville & de tous les amis*
de la chanson. Par C***, du Caveau moderne. Paris: Capelle et Renand,
1811. Contains the first known printing of the melody of *Frère Jacques.*

Anon. **Here We Go Round the Mulberry Bush** *The universal magazine of*
knowledge and pleasure... Vol. XXVII. London: John Hinton, 1760.
Contains the first known printing of *Nancy Dawson*, the tune of which
was later set as *(Here We Go Round the) Mulberry Bush.*

Edward Jones **All Through the Night** *Musical and poetical relicks of the Welsh*
1752–1824, compiler *bards: preserved by tradition, and authentic manuscripts, from remote*
antiquity; never before published. London: Printed for the author, 1784.
First edition; contains the first printing of the music of *All Through the*
Night. The authorship of both words and music is unknown.

George Petrie **Londonderry Air** *The Petrie collection of the ancient music of Ire-*
1789–1866, ed. *land. Arranged for the piano-forte.* Dublin: Printed at the University
Press for the Society for the Preservation and Publication of the
Melodies of Ireland, 1855. First edition; contains the first known printing of the tune later known as *Londonderry Air.*

Niel Gow **The Irish Washerwoman** *A third collection of Strathspey reels &c for*
1727–1807, compiler *the piano-forte, violin, and violoncello.* Edinburgh: Printed for the
author, 1792. First edition; contains the first known printing of *The*
Irish Washerwoman.

Thomas Moore **'Tis the Last Rose of Summer** *A selection of Irish melodies with*
1779–1852, compiler *symphonies and accompaniments by Sir John Stevenson Mus. Doc.*
and characteristic words by Thomas Moore Esqr 5th number. London:
J. Power; Dublin: W. Power, 1813. First edition; contains the first printing of *'Tis the Last Rose of Summer.*

Sebastián Yradier **"Habanera"** *Fleurs d'Espagne chansons espagnoles... Publiées pour*
1809–65 *chant et piano avec texte français et espagnol. Paroles françaises de Taglia-*
fico & P. Bernard. Paris: Heugel & Cie., 1864. First edition. Bizet
adapted the third song, *El ar[r]eglito*, a "chanson havanaise," for the
habanera in *Carmen.*

Georges Bizet *Carmen opéra comique en 4 actes tiré de la nouvelle de Prosper Mérimée*
1838–75 *poéme* [sic] *de H. Meilhac et L. Halévy.... Partition chant et piano*
arrangée par l'auteur. Paris: Choudens père et fils, 1875. First edition of
the piano-vocal score.

Franjo Žaver Kuhač **Marche slave** *Južno-slovjenske narodne popievke. (Chansons*
1834–1911, compiler *nationales des slaves du sud.) Većim ih dielom po narodu sám sakupio,*

ukajdio, glasovirsku pratnju udesio, te izvorni im tekst pridodao Fr. Š. Kuhač. Zagreb: C. Albrecht, 1879. First edition; contains the first known printing of the Serbian folk song used by Tchaikovsky in his Slavonic March *(Marche slave).*

Pyotr Il'yich Tchaikovsky
1840–93

Marche slave [*Slavyanskiy marsh na narodno slavyanskiya temï dlya bol'shago orkestra sochineniye 31.*] Moscow: P. Jurgenson, 1880. First edition of the full score of the Slavonic March.

William Sandys
1792–1874, compiler

The First Noel *Christmas carols, ancient and modern; including the most popular in the west of England, and the airs to which they are sung. Also specimens of French provincial carols.* London: Richard Beckley, 1833. Contains the first known printing of the music and words together of *The First Noel.*

Teodoro Cottrau
1827–79

Santa Lucia *Collezione completa delle canzoncine nazionali napoletane con accompagnamento di pianoforte.* Naples: Stabilimento Musicale Partenopeo successore di B. Girard e Co., 1850 or 1851. The only known copy of the probable first edition of *Santa Lucia;* the words have also been attributed to Cottrau.

John Piersol McCaskey
b. 1837, compiler

Deck the Halls with Boughs of Holly *Franklin Square song collection. Songs and hymns for schools and homes, nursery and fireside.* New York: Harper & Brothers, 1881. First edition; contains the first known printing of the words of *Deck the Halls with Boughs of Holly.* The music was first published in *Musical and poetical relicks of the Welsh bards* (see above, under *All Through the Night*).

Sir Arthur Sullivan
1842–1900

The Mikado. Leipzig: Bosworth & Co., 1893. Sullivan's copy of the first edition of the full score.

Anon.

Gaudeamus igitur *Schauenburg's Allgemeines deutsches Kommersbuch. Ursprunglich herausgegeben unter musikalischer Redaktion von Friedrich Silcher und Friedrich Erk. 81.–85. Auflage.* Lahr: Moritz Schauenburg, 1913 or earlier. Student's songbook, which includes *Gaudeamus igitur;* the upper and lower covers have metal bosses (*Biernägel*) to protect the book from spilled beer.

Johannes Brahms
1833–97

Akademische Fest-Ouvertüre für grosses Orchester ... Op. 80. Partitur. Berlin: N. Simrock, 1881. First edition of the full score of the *Academic Festival Overture.* In the finale, Brahms introduces the familiar student song *Gaudeamus igitur.*

Johann Strauss II
1825–99

The Blue Danube Waltz *An der schönen, blauen Donau. Walzer für das Pianoforte componirt ... Op. 314.* Vienna: C. A. Spina, 1867. Alternative first edition of the waltz *On the Beautiful Blue Danube* arranged for piano (pl. 8).

Program that included Strauss conducting *The Blue Danube Waltz*; Boston, 17 June 1872. This was his first appearance in America.

Jacques Offenbach
1819–80

Cancan   *Orphée aux enfers, opéra bouffon en deux actes et quatre tableaux, paroles de Mr Hector Crémieux ... Partition chant et piano.* Paris: Heugel et Cie., 1858. First edition of the piano vocal score. The *Galop*, as arranged by Manuel Rosenthal, became the *Cancan* in the ballet *Gaîté parisienne* (1938).

Franz Lehár
1870–1948

The Merry Widow   *Die lustige Witwe. Operette in drei Akten (teilweise nach einer fremden Grundidee) von Victor Léon und Leo Stein.... In Szene gesetzt von Victor Léon. Zum ersten Mal aufgeführt am 30. Dezember 1905 im k. k. priv. Theater an der Wien. Vollständiges Soufflierbuch mit sämtlichen Regiebemerkungen.* Vienna: Ludwig Doblinger, 1906 or later. First edition of the mise-en-scène (production book) for *The Merry Widow*.

Sir Noël Coward
1899–1973

"I'll See You Again," from *Bitter Sweet*. London: Chappell & Co., Ltd., 1929. First edition of the sheet music.

✒ Foreign Popular and Folk Music Wall Exhibits

Anon.

God Save the King   *A Loyal Song sung at the Theatres Royal for two voices.* [London: no publisher, 1745.] The earliest known sheet music of *God Save the King*. The authorship of both words and music is unknown.

Claude-Joseph
Rouget de Lisle
1760–1836

La Marseillaise   *Hymne des Marseillois.* In *Annales patriotiques et litteraires*, 29 October 1792 (no. 303). An early printing of *La Marseillaise*, six months after it was composed.

Anon.

O Du Lieber Augustin   *Augustin Favorit-Walzer nach dem Böhmischen.* Leipzig: Breitkopf & Härtel, ca. 1800. The only known copy of the possible first printing of the words and music together of *O Du Lieber Augustin*.

[Franz Xaver Gruber
1787–1863]

Silent Night   *Vier ächte Tyroler-Lieder für Sopran-Solo oder für vier Stimmen mit willkührlicher Begleitung des Piano-Forte gesungen von den Geschwistern Strasser aus dem Zillerthale.* Dresden: A. R. Friese, 1832.

Contains the first edition of *Stille Nacht* (Silent Night); neither Gruber, the composer, nor Joseph Mohr, the author of the words, is mentioned (pl. 9).

New Theatre Royal, Covent Garden
Poster, dated 29 November 1809, announcing *The Exile*, "a grand melo-dramatick opera" by Mr. Mazzinghi, and the farce *Is He a Prince?*

Anon.
God Rest You, Merry Gentlemen *A political Christmas Carol, set to music, to be chaunted or sung throughout the United Kingdom and the dominions beyond the seas, by all persons thereunto moved.* London: William Hone, 1820. Contains the possible first printing of the music and Hone's (parodied) words together of *God Rest You, Merry Gentlemen*. The composer of the music is not known.

Sir Henry R. Bishop
1786–1855
Home! Sweet Home! *Home! Sweet Home! Sung by Miss Tree, in Clari, or The Maid of Milan. Composed, and partly founded on a Sicilian air by Henry R. Bishop.* London: Goulding, D'Almaine, Potter, & Co., 1823. First edition of the sheet music.

Russian poster
Poster for The First Musical and Entertainment Festival, at Novaya Derevnya (a spa in the Crimea), on 3 June 1856.

First editions of music illustrated by famous artists
Pablo Picasso (1881–1973). Igor Stravinsky, *Ragtime*, piano (Paris: Editions de La Sirène, 1919).

Jean Cocteau (1889–1963). Francis Poulenc, *La Voix humaine*, piano-vocal score (Paris: Ricordi, 1959).

Joan Miró (1893–1983). Josep Mestres-Quadreny, *Digodal*, string quartet (Barcelona: Clivis, 1965).

Henri de Toulouse-Lautrec (1864–1901). Désiré Dihau, "Les Vieux Papillons," from *Mélodies de Désiré Dihau* (Paris: C. Joubert, 1895).

Henri Matisse (1869–1954). Paul Arma, "Chant funèbre pour un guerrier," from *Chants du silence* (Paris: Heugel et Cie., 1953).

Salvador Dalí (1904–89). Ernesto Halffter, *Marche joyeuse* (Madrid: Unión Musical Española, 1925). The image is probably a self-portrait.

Kurt Weill
1900–50
"Mack the Knife" "Moritat," from *Die Dreigroschenoper*. Lyrics by Bertolt Brecht. Vienna: Universal-Edition, 1929. First edition of the sheet music; the song is known in English as "Mack the Knife."

Die Dreigroschenoper. Playbill for an early performance; Vienna, Raimund-Theater, 12 May 1929. With *Aufstieg und Fall der Stadt Mahagonny*. Playbill for an early performance with Lotte Lenya; Vienna, Raimund-Theater, [2 May 1932].

The Beatles	A photograph of the four Beatles, with their signatures.
Claude-Michel Schönberg *b. 1941*	"La Faute à Voltaire," from *Les Misérables*. Lyrics by A. Boublil and J. M. Natel. Paris: Editions Musicales Alain Boublil, 1980. First edition of the sheet music from the original Paris production. The song is known in English as "Little People."
Sir Andrew Lloyd Webber *b. 1948*	*The Phantom of the Opera*. Poster for the original production; London, Her Majesty's Theatre, 1986.

James Fuld's Writings on Music

Books

American Popular Music (Reference Book) 1875–1950. Philadelphia: Musical Americana, 1955.

A Pictorial Bibliography of the First Editions of Stephen C. Foster. Philadelphia: Musical Americana, 1957.

With Mary Wallace Davidson. *18th-century American Secular Music Manuscripts: An Inventory.* Philadelphia: Music Library Association, Inc., 1982.

The Book of World-Famous Libretti: The Musical Theater from 1590 to Today. Rev. ed. New York: Pendragon Press, 1994.

The Book of World-Famous Music: Classical, Popular and Folk. 4th ed. New York: Dover Publications, Inc., 1995.

Articles

With Lester S. Levy. "Unrecorded Early Printings of *The Star Spangled Banner.*" *Notes* 27 (1970): 245–51.

"The First Complete Printing of Handel's 'Messiah.'" *Music & Letters* 55 (1974): 454–57.

"Nineteenth-century Operatic Violin Conductors' Scores." *Notes* 31 (1974): 278–80.

"Surrounded by One's Friends." *Notes* 32 (1976): 479–90.

"A Collection of Music Autographs." *Manuscripts* 32 (1980): 12–27.

"Music Programs and Posters: The Need for an Inventory." *Notes* 37 (1981): 520–32.

"Music: Books, Printed Scores, Autographs." *AB Bookman's Weekly* 71 (1983): 1294–1316.

"The Few Known Autographs of Scott Joplin." *American Music* 1 (1983): 41–48.

"Fifty Years of Music Collecting." *AB Bookman's Weekly* 72 (1983): 4115–32.

"The Ricordi 'Libroni.'" In *Festschrift Albi Rosenthal*, ed. Rudolf Elvers. Tutzing: Hans Schneider, 1984, 139–45.

"Experiences While 'Musicologing.'" In *Festschrift Rudolf Elvers*, ed. Ernst Herttrich and Hans Schneider. Tutzing: Hans Schneider, 1985, 199–205.

With Frances Barulich. "Harmonizing the Arts: Original Graphic Designs for Printed Music by World-famous Artists." *Notes* 43 (1986): 259–71.

"Jewish Music Published in Palestine: An Introduction." *Musica Judaica* 10 (1987–88): 70–80.

"Songs from Messiah Published During Handel's Lifetime." *Notes* 45 (1988): 253–57.

With Beverly A. Hamer. "Collecting 20th-century American Popular Music." *AB Bookman's Weekly* 88 (1991): 2289–90.

"American Music in The British Library: A Preliminary Survey." In *Sundry Sorts of Music Books: Essays on The British Library Collections presented to O. W. Neighbour on his 70th Birthday*, ed. Chris Banks, Arthur Searle, and Malcolm Turner. London: The British Library, 1993, 375–84.

With David Hunter. "Collectors and Music Bibliography: A Preliminary Survey." In *Music Publishing and Collecting: Essays in Honor of Donald W. Krummel*, ed. David Hunter. Graduate School of Library and Information Science, University of Illinois at Urbana-Champaign, 1994, 215–33.